How to Cut Costs & Unnecessary Expenses

Published by:

mcHoward Business Coaching
203 S Stratford Rd Ste T
Winston-Salem, NC 27103

LIMITS OF LIABILITY / DISCLAIMER OF WARRANTY:

While the majority of my efforts focus on developing new ways to build your business, it's important to remember that the one guaranteed way of keeping more money in your bank account is by doing everything in your power to cut costs at every available opportunity. Sounds simple, but studies have shown that many businesses operating today are nowhere near maximizing their cost saving opportunities.

In this book you will learn:

Why cost cutting is important!

Where to start!

The benefits of a "Wastage Audit".

How to enroll your staff in cost cutting programs.

Why is cost cutting important?

This may seem like a obvious question, however, there have been countless successful businesses that have failed because they let the costs of operating their business spiral out of control. In fact, some of the biggest global corporate collapses have occurred due to this very reason.

So, if it can happen to billion-dollar corporate giants it can happen to small businesses. It's one of the main reasons why 80% of all businesses fail.

Cost cutting can be a very quick way to boost your bottom line in the short term. By shedding staff or improving the systems in your business you can immediately impact your profitability. Constant focus on cutting costs will encourage you to review your policies and practices more often than you otherwise might consider doing. Another key advantage is that it can improve your ability to raise capital. If you're approaching a bank, angel investor, venture capitalist or even your next-door neighbor, showing that you're constantly focused on cutting costs will be seen in a very favorable light.

Being an effective cost cutter can also shelter you from a downturn in demand for your product or service. It's very easy to live the good life when your business is making good profits. But remember, what goes up must come down. It's simply good business sense to reduce costs at every available opportunity. Last, but certainly not least, is that it keeps you in control. Isn't that what it's all about, being in control of your business and not the other way around?

Where to Start?

Finances

Probably the best place to start is to look at how your business is currently being financed. If you have an overdraft, when was the last time you seriously shopped your business around to different banks? Too many business owners fail to recognize that the banks are now becoming more and more competitive. This means that if you approach a number of different banks (preferably with an up to date business plan) and ask them for the best rates they can offer, you will often find that you can secure cheaper interest rates on your overdraft. If you're in the fortunate situation where you have surplus funds in your business bank accounts, talk to your bank manager about offsetting these funds against your mortgage or depositing them in a short-term, high-interest yielding account.

Suppliers

The same is true of your suppliers. When was the last time you sat down with them and attempted to negotiate better payment terms or an improved volume discount? Remember, it's the squeaky wheel that gets the grease. You should sit down on a regular basis and analyze all of your suppliers. Make sure you competitively quote your suppliers for everything your business needs. You will be amazed how quickly people will negotiate with you. Remember, it costs six times more to find a new client than it does to do business with an existing one. Your suppliers know this and simply asking them for better terms or cheaper rates can save you a lot of money.

Trading hours

Have you ever sat down and had a close look at your hours of operation? There are countless businesses that open too early or stay open too late just because that's what everyone else is doing. Have a closer look at when you're making most of your sales or when you receive most of your customer enquiries, (the daily journal in the Time Management section will help you to track this). Once you have done this for a few weeks, it will become apparent that there are certain time periods that are costing you money simply to be open. For a lot of retail stores this can be between 9 and 10 on a Monday or Tuesday morning. Even if you reduced your work week by these two hours, that can represent a savings of over $1 or $2 thousand dollars over twelve months. Enough for a holiday or a basic website to further promote your business.

Staff remuneration

Is there a better way you can be rewarding your staff? A lot of business owners are now looking at restructuring the way they pay their staff to reduce costs and provide greater incentive for greater output. It's a well-known fact that salespeople have been paid increased commissions based on increased sales for many years, but there are a growing number of astute business owners who are now starting to pay their other non-sales people based on the level of sales an organization generates. This has the effect of having everyone focused on increasing sales, so it becomes a far greater team effort across the board. Companies that have started to do this have noticed an increase in customer satisfaction levels, faster delivery times, more efficient debt collection procedures, greater efficiency in communications, a higher level of office morale and countless other benefits. Is there a way you could look at doing something similar in your business?

Business premises

Where you choose to locate your business will have a major impact on your operating costs. It is one of the most important things to consider, even if your business is well established. When looking at locating or relocating your business it's important to ask the following questions:

- Will customers be coming to the business or will I be going to them?

- If customers are visiting me, what impression do I want to create?

- Where do my customers come from?

- Do they need easy parking facilities?

- Do I need to be highly visible?

- Will I be employing staff?

- Is it easy for staff to find car parking or public transportation?

- How far away are your business premises from where you live?

- Does your business require partitioning? Offices? Storage space?

- Can you access your business premises after hours?

- What is your budget?

- How long is the lease for?

- What happens if I break the lease?

- Is it better to buy the business premises?

- What are the incidental costs? Cleaners? Outgoings, etc?

    When you're thinking of locating your business you need to be very clear on all the above questions.

Eliminate the invisible!

Once you have had a close look at some of the major expenses in your business, its then time to have a very close look at invisible expenses. These are the incidentals you may be spending money on which your customers or staff are indifferent to. A lot of business owners spend money on incidental items that don't really add any value to the business. Have a look at the following list of items and ask yourself if they would really be missed if they disappeared from your business tomorrow.

- Magazines and newspapers

- Expensive tea and coffee

- Couriers and express post services

- Expensive packaging

- What are some of the items in your business you could be living without?

Cost Cutting Tips & Tricks

Cash management

1. Pay no bill before its time. Don't pay any bills until they're due. See who has a late charge, and who doesn't. Send checks out on Friday to take advantage of the weekend "float."

2. Exercise dormant lines of credit. Frequently business owners set up lines of credit they don't use. The bank may drop your line of credit if it is not used for a certain period, so be sure to check their use requirements. If there is an annual cost, such as 1%, many business owners consider dropping a line of credit. But remember the rule of banking: If you really need the money, you probably can't qualify for the loan.

3. If you don't have a line of credit, set one up now. Check around for competitive rates. It's a lot cheaper than using credit cards if you're really in a cash flow pinch.

4. Closely monitor your three sources of cash:

- Payments in process, not yet completed

- Invoices billed out, but not yet collected

- Paid billings: cash on hand

5. Complete and bill out invoices as fast as possible. The sooner they're billed, the sooner they'll pay. We're all tempted to "let the work fill up the time available." But, it delays payment of your bill. If they don't have your invoice, they won't pay the bill.

6. Give your employees a higher fee split if they're willing to wait to be paid until you're paid. This policy can be a substantial help to cash flow problems as the highest percent of expenses is employee payroll.

7. Be very aggressive with past-due accounts, particularly non-institutional companies, such as contractors. Many contractors are expected to make a fair amount of revenue due to the shortage of labor. Let them be late paying someone else, not you. In collections, the "squeaky wheel gets the grease." Call every day if necessary.

8. Get interest on your money by setting up a "sweeps" account or interest-bearing checking account and doing daily deposits. Even if it's only two or three percent interest, it's better than nothing.

9. Get as many advance payments as possible. Offer a discount, if necessary. Require pre-payment from private clients, or business clients that may cause payment problems. If they won't pre-pay or pay half at the beginning of the project, turn down the work. Don't work for free.

Rent - office and storage

10. Renegotiate your lease to a lower rent, or a temporary lower rent while business is slow. If office vacancies are high, your landlord will probably prefer reduced rent to no rent.

11. Sublet unused office space to others in your industry or a complimenting industry. A real estate attorney may lease space to a realtor. Or, move out of your larger office space to a smaller sublet office.

12. If you need to move or downsize to a smaller office, but have a lease, work with your landlord. Maybe he or she will let you sublease, make a partial payment of the rest of your lease, or move to a smaller space. In most parts of the country, the office market is not doing well, and landlords are willing to negotiate. Negotiate with the landlord for some type of compensation for phone and electrical improvements you have made and paid for, but will have to leave behind when you move.

13. Move "back home" and work out of the garage, spare bedroom, or even the dining room table. If you think it's too cramped, consider it only temporary until business picks up again.

14. Shop around for low-cost storage space. We have to save our files for at least 5 years, and many of us save them for much longer. What to keep and throw out in files is an individual decision, but you can shop for a lower storage cost.

15. Get rid of excess stored stuff, such as old office furniture. Sell it or give it away. Don't pay storage costs for things you really don't need. Don't be a packrat.

Pricing

16. Keep close track of your competitor's costs. Don't underbid or lose work because you overbid. When fees are changing, don't get left behind and lose valuable assignments from overbidding, or income from underbidding.

17. Don't offer lower prices to a client that isn't price sensitive. Why give away your profits? Not everyone gives assignments to the low bidder. Some don't even do competitive bidding.

18. Know your costs on appraisals. The high fee jobs may not be the most profitable. It may be more profitable to set up referral alliances with appraisers in other geographic areas, rather than spend the time traveling and doing extra research on an area you're not familiar with.

Dues and publications

19. Carefully review each organization where you pay dues. Do you really participate, or do you send in dues because "you always have." You can always rejoin later, when business picks up if you feel guilty about dropping out.

20. Review the publications you subscribe to. If a publication doesn't really help you in your business, consider not renewing.

Personnel

21. Cut back principals' salaries. Pay yourself last, after paying all other expenses. Although this may seem obvious, many companies have developed serious financial problems because the owners kept taking out large salaries.

22. "Lease" your employees. Instead of laying off an experienced secretary, lease him or her to another company until business picks up again.

23. Use temporary help whenever possible when your business substantially increases. That's how the mortgage lending industry handled the 1991 to 1993 substantial increases in lending volumes. They first let go the temps, then the permanent employees.

24. Use part-time support staff. They don't require benefits and usually have more flexible hours. Laying off a part-timer, or cutting back their hours, is much easier than a long-term loyal, full-time employee.

25. Have a cost cutting brainstorming session with your associates and support staff. If you're working alone, set up a lunch with your accountant or other appraisal business owners to swap ideas. You'll get many ideas you've never thought about before.

26. Have one person attend a seminar, and then later "show and tell" the rest of your staff. For example, we all want to find out about the new USPAP changes, but the seminars are expensive. Just send one person, who gives a "mini-seminar" to your other associates and yourself.

27. Attend only local seminars to eliminate travel costs. If there's an out-of-town seminar you want to take, call the sponsor and see if it will be offered locally. Or see if you can purchase audio cassettes or video tapes.

28. Use an outside payroll service such as Paychex or ADP to cut bookkeeping payroll costs. Or, do it yourself by using a simple software program like Quickbooks. Don't use a CPA to do your bookkeeping.

29. Broaden staff responsibilities. For example, instead of paying an outside bookkeeper, have your secretary do it. If you must lay off a full-time secretary because your work has dropped, consider letting a less experienced associate appraiser do part-time clerical work. At least they'll have some income. Instead of having outside firms do janitorial and delivery services, have your employees do it. It's better than getting laid off, or sitting around worrying about getting laid off.

30. Cut your FICA and FUTA by setting up non-cash compensation, such as a "cafeteria" benefits plan with such benefits as health insurance and paid time off.

31. Use college interns or co-op students for research, setting up databases, etc. They work for credit or a low salary on a short-term basis and can work on specific projects, or on general research.

32. Get free or low-cost consulting from a local college business school's small business consulting programs, or the SBA's SCORE (Senior Corps of Retired Executives) program. They can give you advice on such topics as marketing, collections, and cost accounting.

Insurance

33. Be sure you're not overpaying for workers compensation. How are your appraisers classified? They are relatively low risk for a claim and should be classified as real estate agents or some other category, rather than as much more expensive inspectors. If your insurance company insists on classifying them in a high rate category, change insurers. If this year's workers comp is based on last year's employment, be sure to notify your insurer if this year's payroll is expected to be lower.

34. If you have high production typists, be sure to minimize repetitive stress to avoid workers comp rate increases, if one of them becomes disabled. Contact your workers comp carrier for more information.

35. Look at your auto insurance coverage. Consider dropping collision on older vehicles. If the car is only worth $1,500, why pay $200 per year extra for collision?

36. Raise deductibles on such coverage as auto collision, disability, property/casualty, and liability insurance. For example, have disability insurance "kick in" after 90 days instead of 30 days.

37. Evaluate all your insurance policies for their risk/benefit and decide which ones you think you will really need. Don't over insure.

Taxes

38. Don't overpay your income tax quarterlies. If you anticipate that your taxable income will drop this year, don't pay taxes based on last year's income. Work with your accountant to pay quarterlies based on a more accurate estimate. If you've already overpaid your quarterlies, ask your accountant about a quick refund, using Forms 4466 and 1138.

39. Close to year-end, schedule a tax-planning meeting with your accountant to shift income and expenses. For example, shift income into the next year to decrease this year's taxes.

Office supplies

40. Shop for the best prices. Don't pay too much attention to percent discount. Look at the bottom line. No one pays full retail. Purchasing supplies in bulk may be worthwhile.

41. Use office warehouse companies like Office Club. They usually offer the lowest prices. Many will deliver. Don't forget discount stores like Price Club, Wal-Mart, and Costco. Many carry some of the most-purchased office supplies, like paper, pens, and laser jet cartridges. You don't always need to buy brand names.

42. Keep close track of inventory so you don't have to pay someone to "run over" to the nearby high-priced office supply store.

43. Lock the supply cabinet. Yes, this will cause grumbling. Explain that it will keep it neater, and you'll be less likely run out of supplies.

44. Scan a PDF to your email instead of using U.S. mail whenever possible. It's cheaper and faster.

45. Use the back side of old copies for rough drafts to cut your paper costs.

46. Cut "post-it" pads into smaller sizes to use for page markers. Or, have your photo processor do it.

Equipment and phones

47. Sell or donate excess office furniture and equipment. Storage space is expensive. You can sell it to employees, the public, or the vendor (on consignment). Donate it to local charities or schools.

48. When leasing equipment, get an option to cancel due to closure or consolidation. Don't get an "evergreen clause", where the contract always continues unless you give 30 days' notice. They are difficult to cancel, as the expiration date is hard to monitor.

49. Renegotiate your equipment leases. For example, change to a smaller copier. Buy shorter maintenance agreements, so that, for example, if your copier volume is lowered, you can decrease maintenance. See if you really need all your service contracts. Maybe it's better to pay for repairs on an ad hoc basis.

50. Reduce phone lines. If you have fewer staff, you need fewer phone lines. Cancel some of the optional features you don't really need.

51. Watch the data usage on your cell phones. Make sure you are using WiFi as often as possible when streaming video on sites like YouTube. Also make sure you are staying within your data limits when texting.

Here are some additional considerations...

1. Go Green (Smartly)

Cost Cutting Tip: Most companies think that going green will cost them money, but it's important to remember that greening is first and foremost about conservation - doing more with less. Though you may spend a little more on eco-friendly products, like paper with recycled content, you'll reduce operational costs by reductions in paper use and other areas, like energy, water and travel, therefore, saving money overall.

2. Virtual Support

Cost Cutting Tip: Go with virtual contractors for your administrative staff (and other staff if possible). With virtual assistants you don't have to pay for extra space, buy or upkeep equipment or software, you can skip payroll expenses and benefits, and you pay for only what you need.

3. Spending Wisely on Advertising

Cost Cutting Tip: When you do advertise in publications, include a coupon to test the responses to your ad.

4. Free Conference Calls

Cost Cutting Tip: Try using FreeConfrenceCall.com or one of the many other free tele-conference services. Not only are these services free (they make their money through rebates issued by the phone company) they are great for more than just business. For example, Free Conferencing Corporation has case studies of families using this free conference call service for reunions, wedding planning, religious services, and planning friends weekend.

5. Cheap Office Space

Cost Cutting Tip: Can't afford to rent much needed office space? Try reaching out to tenants of existing space. Ask for a few desks in their space, in exchange for taking over the office cleaning responsibilities. A lot of people have extra space that they are committed to. So, a simple barter exchange like this can be a huge win-win.

6. Join A Trade Exchange

Cost Cutting Tip: One of the best methods of preserving cash and generating revenue (better than cutting costs) is for a small business to become a member of a trade exchange. One of our clients has a company that's a charter member of James River Trade Exchange. JRTE handles all the reporting to IRS and they have many businesses that provide products and services that fulfill our client's business needs, which they can buy with trade dollars earned by providing their services to JRTE customers, the vast majority of whom we would not otherwise have had the opportunity to do business with. Barter is a no-brainer for most small businesses.

7. Downsize Your Office Space

Cost Cutting Tip: Move files and storage offsite so you can fit in a smaller office space. Storage costs are much less in a giant warehouse than they are in your office. We did this and got rid of 15 file cabinets worth of files that we rarely access (but can't ditch!). But don't stop there! Consider having employees tele-commute to save space for you and gas dollars for them. And how about that big lobby - do you really need all that space for your few walk in customers?

8. Go VOIP

Cost Cutting Tip: Switch to VOIP for your phone system. We got rid of our expensive phone service base costs, costs per long-distance phone call, and system maintenance fees associated with your phone system and switched to a VOIP system. The upfront costs were minimal (set up of service and purchase of hard phones and soft phone software) and we now have a low monthly cost and free calling. The system paid for itself in 9 months- and after that it's been just cheap calling forever!

9. Interns

Cost Cutting Tip: I find people looking to build their portfolio, resume or just to get their foot in the door and barter services. I always have an intern from the local high school that comes in and helps us out and my labels were all designed by a recent grad from art school.

10. Use Facebook instead of Business Cards

Cost Cutting Tip: The design and printing of business cards can be expensive. Facebook has really stepped up their game in the business space when it comes to the communication tactics a business needs to run operations. Instead of offering a business card when you meet someone, get their name and connect with them on Facebook. This has two important benefits. One, they get to know about your business when you request them to like your business page. Second, a connection means a messenger connection. You do not need a phone number to call someone in Facebook...just the connection. You can call anyone you are connected to through messenger and you can send messages within messenger as well. These two benefits eliminate the need to share an email or phone number when you don't have a business card available.

11. Make Good Decisions

Cost Cutting Tip: How many decisions do you and your employees make each day? Each one represents an opportunity to be unproductive and/or ineffective depending on how easily and how well you make those decisions. For major improvement, focus on the decisions. Eliminate the unnecessary decisions and get good at the necessary decisions.

12. Simply Do It Faster

Cost Cutting Tip: The cost I cut was my time. Instead of providing 40 minutes per coaching call, I reduced it to 30 minutes. With less time we both focus better and now I can add another client to my daily calendar. Same results, less time, more money.

13. Cut the Advertising & Get Social

Cost Cutting Tip: Cut newspaper advertising and consumer shows in favor of social networking sites, viral marketing and workshops whenever possible. Facebook has targeting tools that work better than a mailing list for direct mail. You can now target interests and you can invest as little as $1 a day!

14. Cheap Website (But Not Cheap Looking)

Cost Cutting Tip: Have your web designer build the site with WordPress. It will look great and you can keep it up to date yourself. You can also build a decent looking website with GoDaddy in under an hour and about $20 a month.

15. Smart Marketing Strategy

Cost Cutting Tip: Track the results of your marketing efforts by including a specific offer they can't refuse and a clear call to action telling how to take advantage of the offer, along with a coupon, download, subscription, special code, or other low-cost device you can track to discover what works best. Then change or ditch anything that doesn't generate enough leads or sales.

16. Get in Their Face

Cost Cutting Tip: Referrals are the best source of strong clients... visit every networking organization in your area (Chambers of Commerce, BNI groups, Rotary, etc.) and introduce yourself, your business, and your quality. Most organizations allow you to visit at least two times before expecting you to join. Some never do. Nothing will sell your business more than a highly engaged owner out discussing business. Make sure to return the referral favors as much as possible.

17. Source with Disabled Organizations

Cost Cutting Tip: We work with a client who partners with a local non-profit disabled organization to assemble and package their jewelry. They get excellent quality; low cost work and the positive feedback has been tremendous.

18. Jump Start the Accounting

Cost Cutting Tip: Save thousands of dollars in accounting fees by having a specific date by which you get your accounting data to your accountant. Most accounting firms have a slower time in the very beginning of the month. By agreeing to get your work to them by (for example) the third of each month, you often get reduced rates in your accounting maintenance fees. You will have more information in a timely basis and they fill in the weaker hours of their practice.

19. Recycle

Cost Cutting Tip: Work with your suppliers to recycle packing materials. Raw materials often come packaged with foam separators which the supplier won't take back and which most businesses have no use for, so they typically get thrown away. Create cardboard separators and remove them during production, then return to your supplier for re-use. This results in a cost savings for your supplier and you can often negotiate a reduction in material costs.

20. No Paper = No Cost

Cost Cutting Tip: Go paperless! Don't print it. You can get an eFax number to send and receive everything electronically. Don't print it out - file it electronically. Share drafts of documents, designs, etc. electronically. Use e-mail or an online project management tool like Google Docs or Base Camp to share and comment on documents. If you don't have to buy paper, envelopes, postage, file folders, ink or maintain your printer/fax - you can save hundreds of dollars per year - even in a small office. Plus - you're going GREEN!

21. It's All About Your Temperature

Cost Cutting Tip: Install a programmable thermostat and set it at reasonable temperatures. Program the thermostat to 50 degrees at night and over the weekends and 70 degrees during the day in winter. Set the thermostat to move to its daytime temperature 2 hours before you arrive at work to make sure that it's comfortable when you get there. You can often cut your energy costs in half this winter doing this.

22. Talk About Smart, Simple & Easy

Cost Cutting Tip: Brown bag it. Bring your own lunch every day.

23. They're Smarter Than You

Cost Cutting Tip: To figure out the less obvious expenses, be sure to involve your employees. They're on the front lines every day and they often have a better idea of what can be cut, dropped or eliminated. For example, maybe they've noticed that you have an incoming paper supply that could be reduced.

24. Make It In 4D

Cost Cutting Tip: Use the 4D method to manage your email (Ditch, Deal, Delegate, Decide). Then run your daily work plan through Outlook Calendar and TaskPad side by side. This will significantly improve your productivity.

25. The Interns Are Social Mavens

Cost Cutting Tip: Hire interns who are experts at Social Networking (Twitter, Instagram, Facebook, LinkedIn) to help with your website launch and your marketing campaigns.

26. This One Rings True

Cost Cutting Tip: Let a bell or buzzer at the front door be your receptionist.

27. Free Admission

Cost Cutting Tip: If you want to attend a business/networking event, there's a way to save on admission fees. Ask organizers if they're looking for volunteer help: setting up tables before the event, greeting people at the door, binding handouts etc. That will get you free admission.

28. Look at That Mug

Cost Cutting Tip: Have employees bring in a favorite mug to have their coffee in instead of purchasing disposable cups.

29. Let Them Eat

Cost Cutting Tip: Seems contradictory, but it's effective. Buy your employees free food for lunch and dinner. They stay a few hours later and save a trip out of the office for lunch. Even more effective - buy food from Costco! For less than $15 worth of food you may get more than $300 in additional productivity.

30. Smarts 101

Cost Cutting Tip: Before attending ANY event on behalf of YOUR business, ask yourself "As the person responsible for this company would I authorize it as a justifiable business expense that I would approve."

31. Bottom Line Productivity

Cost Cutting Tip: Cutting costs in business without cutting capabilities and performance is achieved by optimizing each employee's time. Is every employee spending the majority of his or her day "on the revenue line" - work that generates revenue for the firm? How to do this: have employees keep a time log, then analyze how much time is spent on non-revenue producing activities. Replace those activities with revenue generating activities.

32. Sharpen the Pencil

Cost Cutting Tip: Negotiate. In tough economic times, vendors are often willing to work with long term, loyal customers. If you can pay early, ask for a discount. If you can't pay on time, ask for an extension to stretch out cash flow. You have nothing to lose and everything to gain by asking.

Your pathway to profitability has been set. The only thing you must do now is execute. Please let me know if this is something you would like me to help you with! I also specialize in maximizing profit through the finance side of the business. I can look at your profit & loss statements and determine your breakeven point and tell you if your business is healthy and moving in the right direction. Please connect with me on Facebook and LinkedIn. I am available for consulting and speaking opportunities.

Antonio McCoy 336-575-9920

coachantonio@me.com